THE SEVEN ECUMENICAL COUNCILS

Howard A. Slaatte
Marshall University

University Press
of America™

Books by the Author

Time and Its End

Fire In The Brand

The Pertinence of the Paradox

The Paradox of Existentialist Theology

Modern Science and the Human Condition

The Arminian Arm of Theology

The Dogma of Immaculate Perception

Discovering Your Real Self

iii

TABLE OF CONTENTS

Councils or synods may be traced back to the second half of the second century A.D., when sundry churches in Asia Minor held consultations about the rise of Montanism.[1] Their precise origin is disputed.

The Roman Catholic view is that they were apostolic though not prescribed by divine law, and the apostolic precedent is the "council" of Jerusalem. (Acts 15; Galatians 2.) This would hardly seem to have been a council for it was a meeting at which the Antioch delegates were heard but apparently had no vote, the decision resting solely with the mother church at Jerusalem.

Earlier Protestant writers have stated that synods were of apostolic origin or the outcome of the need of leaders to take counsel together and perhaps modelled according to the secular, provincial assemblies.

The councils of the second century had no fixed geographical limits for membership, nor did they possess an authority which removed the independence of the local church. In the third century the right to vote was limited to the bishops. This was an outgrowth of the idea that each church should have one bishop, who was the sole legitimate successor of the apostles and the official organ of the Holy Spirit.

Later the synods met at regular intervals, and the council of Nice commanded that semi-annual synods be held in every province. This was altered in 692 when the Trullian Council reduced this to one a year.

Earlier ecumenical councils were summoned to combat heresy and schism. The Seven Ecumenical Councils dealt with various matters, some doctrinal, others disciplinary. There are seven councils admitted by the Greek and Latin churches as ecumenical. The Roman Catholics add twelve to this list.[2]

1

An ecumenical council may be defined as "a synod the decrees of which have found acceptance by the Church in the whole world."[3] This does not imply that representatives from the entire church are essential. The whole Christian world accepted this definition until the time of the division of the East and West. The East has maintained this definition; however, the Roman Catholic Church made a new definition, then proceeded to hold several synods regarded as ecumenical but which have been disputed even by Roman Catholic theologians. The dispute lies in the fact that the decrees of such synods as Trent and the Vatican have never been accepted by about half the Christian world.[4]

In order to justify as ecumenical these non-ecumenical councils the modern Roman writers have formulated a new definition: "Ecumenical councils are those to which the Bishops and others entitled to vote are convoked from the whole world under the Presidency of the Pope or his legates, and the decrees of which, having received Papal confirmation, bind all Christians."[5]

It becomes apparent that by accepting the latter definition, at least one of the seven undisputed ecumenical councils would have to be rejected, namely, the I Council of Constantinople; therefore, the writer can accept only the former definition that an ecumenical council is a synod, the decrees, mandates, ordinances or doctrines of which the entire Christian Church has accepted. Regardless of the number of bishops present, the main factor is the universal acknowledgement of the council's decisions. Historically, this is what the recognized Seven Ecumenical Councils have in common, which distinguishes them from all other councils.

> "The Ecumenical Councils claimed for
> themselves an immunity from error in
> their doctrinal and moral teaching,
> resting such claim upon the promise of
> the presence and guidance of the Holy

2

Ghost. The Council looked upon
itself, not as revealing any new
truth, but as setting forth the
faith once for all delivered to
the Saints, its decisions therefore
were in themselves ecumenical, as
being an expression of the mind of
the whole body of the faithful both
clerical and lay, the sensus
communis[6] of the church. And by the
then teaching of the Church that
ecumenical consensus was considered
free from the suspicion of error,
guarded, (as was believed) by the
Lord's promise that the gates of hell
should not prevail against his
Church. This then is what the
Catholics mean when they affirm the
infallibility of the Ecumenical
Councils. Whether this opinion is
true or false is a question outside
the scope of the present discussion.
It was necessary, however, to state
that these Councils looked upon themselves as divinely protected in their
decisions from error in faith and
morals, lest the reader should other-
wise be at a loss to understand the
anathematisms which follow the
decrees..."[7]

-II-

Each of the seven councils was called by
rulers. In the case of I Constantinople the Pope
knew nothing of the matter. Apparently, there was
no consultation with the Pope concerning I Nice.
Regarding the Council of Chalcedon, he gave "a
reluctant consent after the Emperor Marcian had
already convoked the synod." Historically, it is
evident that the See of Rome did not determine the
summoning of the ecumenical councils, neither by
consent nor knowledge.

Extant documents indicate that the idea of

3

Rome's infallibility was unknown, and the confirmation
by the emperor was sought and spoken of in stronger
terms. That it is a historical fact that each of
the Seven Ecumenical Councils eventually found Rome's
approval does not prove that it was regarded as
essential.[8]

Each of the Seven Councils intimated its
relation to the Roman See:

> "1. The First Council of Nice passed a
> canon in which some at least of the Roman
> rights are evidently looked upon as being
> exactly on the same plane as those of
> other metropolitans, declaring that they
> rest upon "custom."
> "It was the Emperor who originated
> this council and called it together...
> Eustathius, bishop of Antioch, presided
> at this council.
> "The matter, however, is of little
> moment as no one would deny the right
> of the See of Rome to preside in a
> council of the whole Church.
> "2. The Second Ecumenical Council was
> called together by the Emperor without
> the knowledge of the Roman Pontiff. Nor
> was he invited to be present. Its first
> president was not in communion at the
> time of its session with the Roman Church.
> And without any recourse to the first of
> all the patriarchs, it passed a canon
> changing the order of the patriarchates,
> and setting a new see of Constantinople in
> a higher place than the other ancient
> patriarchates, in fact immediately
> after Rome. Of course Protestants will
> consider this matter of very minor importance,
> looking upon all patriarchal divisions
> and ranks and priority (the Papacy in-
> cluded) as of a disciplinary character
> and as being jure ecclesiastica[9]
> and in no way affecting doctrine, but
> any fair reading of the third canon of

this synod would seem plainly to
assert that as the first rank of Rome
rested upon the fact of its being the
capital city, so the new capital city
should have the second rank. If this
interpretation is correct it affects
very materially the Roman claim of
jure divino primacy[10]

  "3. Before the third of the
Ecumenical Synods was called to meet,
Pope Celestine had already convicted
Nestorius of heresy and deposed and
excommunicated him. When subsequently
the synod was assembled, and before the
papal legates had arrived, the Council
met, treated Nestorius as in good
standing, entirely ignoring the sentence
already given by Rome, and having examined
the case (after summoning him three
times to appear that he might be heard in
his own defence), proceeded to sentence
Nestorius, and immediately published
the sentence. On the 10th of July (more
than a fortnight later), the papal legates
having arrived, a second session was held,
at which they were told of what had been
done, all of which they were good enough
to approve of.

  "4. The Council of Chalcedon refused to
consider the Eutychian matter as settled
by Rome's decision or to accept Leo's
Tome without examination as to whether it
was orthodox. Moreover, it passed a
canon at a session which the Papal legates
refused to attend, ratifying the order of
the Patriarchates fixed at I Constantinople,
and declaring that "the Fathers had very
properly given privileges to Old Rome as
the imperial city, and that now they gave
the same (τὰ ἴσα πρεσβεῖα) privileges"
to Constantinople as the seat of the
government at that time.

  "5. The fifth of the ecumenical Synods
refused to receive any written doctrinal

5

communication from the then pope (Vigilius),
took his name from the diptychs, and refused
him communion.
"6. The Third Council of Constantinople,
the sixth of the Ecumenical Synods, excommunicated Pope Honorius, who had been
dead for years, for holding and teaching the
Monothelite [11] heresy.
"7. It is certain that the Pope had nothing
to do with the calling of the Seventh Synod,
and quite possible that it was presided
over by Tarasius and not by the Papal
legates."[12]

There is no need of setting forth an elaborate
proof of why the number of ecumenical councils are
limited to seven. St. Gregory in referring to Nice,
I Constantinople, Ephesus and Chalcedon stated that
he venerated these four councils with the Four Gospels.
No one has questioned them. Of the fifth and sixth
almost the same can be said, there being a little
trouble at first about the reception of the fifth.
"The ecumenical character of the seventh is not
disputed by East or West and has not been for near a
thousand years, and full proof of its ecumenicity
will be found in connection with that council."

The reasons for other councils not being listed
as ecumenical may largely be seen in connection with
their canons. In some cases the decrees were not
accepted in the East.[13] The ecumenicity of the
councils is based on the universal acceptance of
their established creeds and canons rather than on
the universality of representation.

Inasmuch as canons were important results of
the councils, it might be well to come to an understanding of the ecclesiastical use of term "canon".
The term derived from the Greek word $\kappa\alpha\nu\iota\nu$ originally
meant "a straight rod" or a "line". Its religious
applications begin with St. Paul's use of it in
II Corinthians 10:13,15 where he uses the term to
mean "prescribed sphere of apostolic work" and in

6

Galations 6:16 where he uses the term to mean "a
regulative principle of Christian life." Clement
of Rome uses it as "a measure of Christian attain-
ment" (Ep. Cor. 7), Irenaeus calls the baptismal
creed "the canon of truth" (i 9,4): Polycrates
(Euseb. v.24) and probably Hippolytus (ib. v.28)
calls it "the canon of faith." Eusebius in his
Ecclesiastical History speaks of "the canon of
truth" (iv. 23), and the "canon of preaching"
(iii. 32). Socrates referred to the Nicene Creed
as a "canon", (ii. 27). Eusebius also refers to
"the ecclesiastical canon" which acknowledged no
more than the four Gospels (vi. 25). Athanasius
referred to "canonized" books as books recognized
by the Church as Holy Scripture, (Fest. Ep. 39).
Eusebius in vi. 3 refers to Clement of Alexandria
as having written a book against Judaizers known as
"The Church's Canon." Athanasius applies the term
"canon" to Church laws. The term has also been
used to mean a clerical body. The Council of
Trent used the term to mean doctrine and law. The
modern tendency has been to limit the term "canon"
to ecclesiastical matters of discipline.[14] This
will be the use made of the term in this discourse.

     In the same sense, the term "creed" is very
important. The term, according to Webster, originated
in "credo", the "I believe" at the beginning of
the Apostles' and Nicene Creeds. Ecclesiastically,
a creed is "a brief, authoritative formula of
religious belief" or "a summary of principles or
opinions professed or adhered to." It is, then, a
composite statement of various doctrines. A
"doctrine", in turn, is a prepared statement,
"that which is taught; a tenet." This becomes a
dogma when it is a tenet or doctrine enforced by
authority.

                        III

     Before giving separate consideration to each
of the seven ecumenical councils it will be
necessary to secure a glimpse of the historical,
Roman setting.

                         7

Early in the fourth century Emperor
Diocletian's plans for an undisputed successor to
the imperial seat failed. When he and his co-
emperor in the West retired in 305 A.D., after
ruling twenty years, there were several candidates
to take their places. Constantine, a contestant for
imperial power, appealed to a strong minority of
Christians which could not be exterminated even
under Diocletian's persecutions.

After a military victory near Rome, Constantine
and his colleague, Licinius, issued jointly the
Edict of Milan in the spring of 313.[15]   Making
Christianity legal, this paved the way for a state
religion in Rome and the epoch in church history
known as the period of the ecumenical councils.[16]
The two emperors soon became engaged in a way for
supremacy, the outcome of which was in favor of
Constantine, who then became the sole emperor in
325 A.D. [17]

Constantine was born 274 A.D. Soldiers pro-
claimed him Augustus at his father's death in 306.
His mother was a Christian and his father favored
Christianity. Constantine took possession of
Britain, Gaul, and Spain. After a campaign against
Maxentius he became "master of Italy" in October,
312. It was before this great battle at the
Milvian Bridge that he saw in the noon day heavens
a vision of a cross with the inscription τούτω νίκα
("by this conquer") exhorting him to conquer by it.[18]
This incident is impressively related by Eusebius,
the first Christian historian, in his Life of
Constantine, having learned of it directly from the
emperor.[19] Socrates also refers to it.[20] The
experience re-enforced Constantine's regard for
Christianity, bringing the affairs of the Western
Church into legal recognition. Christianity
continued to win the respect of the Roman government,
eventuating in Caesaro-papalism when the emperor
became the head of the Church, supported by most
bishops. Accordingly, European rulers for centuries
dictated principles of religion to their subjects,
a practice not climaxed until the Reformation. [21]

In order to gain a coherent historical view of

8

the first council it is necessary to take note of
the predisposing factors which made the council
almost inevitable. The matter that was foremost in
gaining attention among Roman Christians in A.D.
313 was the Donatist schism. This disturbance
began in 312 in Africa. Donatus was the leader of
this party of puritans. As the first in Christian
history "to invoke the interference of secular
power", they appealed to Constantine. They were
later condemned at the Council of Arles in 314.
It was at this council (not ecumenical) that
baptism in the name of the Trinity was made valid
even if conferred by heretics.[22]

During this affair the church in the East
remained quiet. In the midst of the rapid development of ceremonials in worship, the publication
of the Arian heresy[23] began to arouse increased
controversy. This doctrine "threatened the
foundations of the faith and shook the empire for
fifty years."

Arius, the founder of Arianism, was born in
Libya about 256 A.D. and was educated in Antioch,
ordained deacon in Alexandria by Peter, and later
excommunicated for joining the Meletian schism.
He was received back in communion in 313 upon re-
canting his errors. He was then ordained to priesthood. Arius' heresy did not relate to the incarnation but to the being of God. Several years
later his followers began to teach "the imperfect
humanity of Christ." Arius took exception to the
subject of the triune Godhead.[24] To him, the Father
was God and the Son a creature of the Father, a
secondary God, a mediary being between God and the
world, yet a being created before the world and
before time -- the $\lambda \acute{o} \gamma o s$.

Socrates, an early Christian historian, quotes
Arius as having said, "If the Father begat the Son,
He that was begotten had a beginning of existence;
and from this it is evident, that there was a time
when the Son was not. It therefore necessarily
follows, that he had his subsistence from nothing."[25]
($^{\prime}H v \ \delta \tau \epsilon \ o \acute{u} \kappa \ \acute{\eta} v$). Roots of this doctrine may be
traced back to Origen[26] of the third century.

Arius was anathematized in 321 A.D. Of those who had given him active support Eusebius, bishop of Nicomedia, was the most prominent. Eusebius of Ceasarea, who later became the eminent church historian, was a less enthusiastic abettor of Arius.

The orthodox opposed this Subordinationism charging it to be a polytheism, so the new doctrine of the person of Christ became the source of controversy which proved too vital to be set aside, for it involved the very foundations of Christianity -- the nature of God and the incarnation.[27]

Though orthodoxy eventually triumphed, Arianism gave rise to the first two Councils. It was a doctrine somewhat similar to modern Unitarianism, which ascribes the deity in a type of Sabellianism, a subordination of the Son to the Father though both are of the same essence.

IV

It was at this time that Constantine perceived that the Church needed unity both in spirit and in form.[28] Heresy and schism would solve nothing. Local church councils failed to secure a stable unity and harmony of doctrine. In an attempt to better the situation Constantine called the Council of Arles in 314. It must not be overlooked that this council is noteworthy for "establishing the precedent of the calling by the emperor of a great Church Council."[29]

Encouraged by this former action, Constantine summoned the first general council of the entire Christian Church. It was to determine the Arian question. As Elmer T. Merrill suggests, it is not likely that Constantine, like Henry the Eighth of England, aspired to be a theologian, but his desire was to see heresy and orthodoxy determined by the majority.

It may be noted that the General Council of Nice initiated the idea of "a supreme legislative authority for the whole Church"; however, though

10

the Nicene fathers invoked the guidance of the
Holy Spirit, none of them claimed that the
council's acts were infallible or immutable. That
theory developed later.[30]

The immediate incentive for calling this
council was the problem concerning the time for
celebrating Easter. Upon the advice of ecclesias-
tics, Constantine[31] convoked all the bishops in the
empire for the Council at Nice (the modern Isnik),
Bithynia, Asia Minor. This city was a lively,
commercial town convenient to the emperor's own
residence at Nicomedia and accessible by land and
sea.[32] The council consisted of 318 bishops,
besides many priests, deacons, and acolytes, most
of whom were from the East.[33]

Bishops began to assemble May 20, A.D. 325,
and Constantine formally opened the council on
June 19th. Descriptions of this elaborate opening
of the council are given us by Eusebius in his
Life Of Constantine, and by Socrates,[35] Sozomenus[36]
and Theodoret[37] in their respective ecclesiastical
histories. Being absent, the Bishop of Rome was
represented by two priests. Alexander, the Pope
of Alexandria, became considerably involved in the
Arian controversy.[38] Bishop Eusebius of Nicomedia
presided.

There were three parties represented in the
debates of the session: 1. the Catholics, the
term "Catholic" beginning to imply the orthodoxy
which signifies universality in time and place.
Athanasius was the leader of this group, who
attended the council with Alexander, though he was
not a member of the council. 2. the Arians, who
maintained that the Son is a creation of God, not
equal to God, changeable, and essentially "different"
(ετεροδσιος   ) from the Father, the Heterousiasts.
3. the Eusebians, later known as Semi-Arians or
Homoiousians. Their leader was Eusebius of Nicomedia,
who was prone to think in similar but less specific
terms than Arius. They believed the Son was
"of like substance" (ομοιοσιος) with the Father.[39]

The debates soon caused Arianism to appear as a

11

heresy which denied the divinity of Christ, thus
labeling it for condemnation; however, the
Eusebians managed to escape this for they con-
sented "to accept any statement in Scripture,
putting their own interpretation on it, and protested
against any phraseology that was metaphysically
definite."

Finally, Athanasius, chose the term ὁμοούσιος
meaning "of the same essence" as the proper des-
cription of the Father and Son relation, the Son
being the "unfolding of the divine nature" rather
than "the creation of the divine will." This was
the definition established in the Nicene Creed.
The term had been used before by the Sabellians,
who denied any personality distinctions in the
Godhead; but the council insisted that "identity of
essence involved no denial of differentiation of
persons", laying a basis for the expression of the
incarnation.[40] The Father and Son were of the same
essence, but different persons.

The chief result of this council, therefore,
was the establishment of the doctrine of incarnation,
the true divinity of Christ and the identity of
essence between the Father and the Son. Referring
to the significance of this action Shaff states,

> "The fundamental importance of this
> dogma, the number, learning, piety and
> wisdom of the bishops, many of whom
> still bore the marks of the Diocletian
> persecution, the personal presence of
> the first Christian emperor, of Eusebius,
> "the Father of church history", and of
> Athanasius, "the father of orthodoxy"
> (though at the time only archdeacon),
> as well as the remarkable character of
> this epoch, combined in giving to this
> first general synod a peculiar weight
> and authority. It is styled emphatically,
> "the great and holy council" holds the
> highest place among all councils, especial-
> ly with the Greeks, and still lives in
> the Nicene Creed; which is second in
> authority only to the ever venerable

Apostles' Creed."[41]

The creed set forth by the I Council of Nice
in definite language speaks of Christ as the Son
of God "of one essence" (ὁμοούσιον   ) with the
Father, "begotten" (γεννηθέντα) of the Father,
"came down from heaven and was incarnate" for man's
salvation, suffered, rose again, and ascended into
heaven." He is also spoken of as coming again "to
judge the quick and the dead." The creed also includes an anathema against anyone who says,
"Once He was not", or "He came into existence out
of nothing", or "the Son of God is of another substance or essence", or is created, or mutable.[42]

All bishops subscribed to this creed except
Arius, Eusebius of Nicomedia and four others. Three,
including Eusebius changed their minds, and the
other three were exiled into Illyria.[43] The Nicene
Creed was not settled in its final form until the
second general council. This form does not include
the later Latin insertion "filioque" meaning "and
the Son".[44] It must not be overlooked here, that
the creed includes a statement of belief in the
Holy Spirit, but the affirmation that "He proceedeth
from the Father" was not included until the second
general council. The statment that "He proceedeth
from the Father and the Son," with which the
Western Christians are familiar, is thought to have
been added by a council in Spain sometime during the
latter part of the sixth century; however, it is
even today regarded by the Churches in the East as
schismatic or practically heretical.[45]

Upon examining the Nicene Creed it becomes
noteworthy that there is no reference made to the
virgin birth of Christ.[46] Various possible reasons
for this may be developed: 1. the idea may have
been so universally believed that it was not a
subject of debate, 2. it was possibly considered
unessential, or 3. the strength of the idea might
have developed later. The second of these arguments
seems the most feasible to the writer of this
discourse.

The Council also issued an encyclical letter
for the purpose of informing the clergy and laity of

the Church of Alexandria and Christians throughout Egypt, Pentopolis, and Lybia as well as all nations represented at the Council of Nice, of the proceedings and considerations of the synod.[47]

Various disciplinary measures were dealt with during the Council, which resulted in the passing of at least twenty canons. The most important of these canons concerned "the rights of metropolitans, the time of Easter, and the validity of heretical baptism."[48] Canon VI provides that the bishops of Alexandria and Antioch will have the same patriarchal jurisdiction in their respective areas as exercised by the Bishop of Rome. It states, "Let the ancient customs prevail."[49] The doctrine of papal supremacy was apparently unknown to the members of the Nicene Council.[50] There were five metropolitans having oversight of the bishops of a province. These were the bishops of Rome, Alexandria, Antioch, Constantinople and Ephesus. This canon also granted the metropolitans power to determine who could be a bishop in the province of his jurisdiction, "provided it be in accordance with the canons by the suffrage of the majority."[51] Canon XIX provides for the rebaptism of the followers of Paul of Somosata, the anti-Trinitarian.[52]

Other less important canons were enacted which included prohibitions against self-castrated clergy, neophyte presbyters, women living in a presbyter's house, restoration of excommunicated clergy by another bishop, ordination without examination, return to military service, transference of clergymen, and usury practiced by clergymen.[53]

There were other canons besides the above prohibitions. These provided for the election of a bishop by other bishops, the recognition of the bishop of Jerusalem, the deposition of lapsed clergymen, indulgences for prostrators for twelve years, communion for the dying, fallen catechumens becoming but hearers, and standing prayer on the Lord's Day and at Pentecost.[54]

The decision with reference to the Easter question was similar to that of the Council of Arles, except that the Bishop of Alexandria was ordered to

make the annual announcement of the celebration of
Easter instead of the Bishop of Rome. Henceforth
the keeping of Easter was to be on the nearest
Sunday to the exact date rather than on the third
day after the 14th of Nisan, which was commemorated
as the Modern Good Friday.[55]

Miletius, the bishop of Antioch, was admitted
to communion and was allowed to retain his bishopric.
He had formerly been an Arian, but after being
elected by the Antiochian church in 361 he professed
the Nicene Creed. This schism of a half century
finally came to an end.[56]

Eusebius of Nicomedia confessed his inconsistent
subscription to the Nicene Creed. This resulted
in his excommunication soon after the Council ad-
journed.[57] At the close of the council all the
bishops were royally entertained at a banquet[58]
sponsored by the great Emperor Constantine in his
palace. This, being on the 29th of July, fell on the
twentieth anniversary of his accession. Remunerating
them almost lavishly, he congratulated the bishops
for their accomplishments.

This "first and most venerable of ecumenical
synods, and next to the apostolic council at
Jerusalem the most important of all councils of
Christendom" came to a dramatic close. It was the
most important event of the fourth century, an
"epoch in the history of doctrine"[59]   which consummated
all previous discussions on the deity and incarnation
of Christ, thus furthering the development of
orthodox Christendom.

The East did not accept the Council of Nice's
accomplishments with a unanimity such as was seen
in the West; rather it continued to have strong
disagreements. Constantine's plans did not secure
the unity that was anticipated. Constantine even
"veered around from Nice to the favouring of Arianism,
though he finally died in what must now be called the
orthodox faith." His Christian successors also
were inconsistent in their allegiance to orthodoxy.
Valens, for instance, was an Arian; nevertheless,
Theodosius was a sincere Nicene.[60]

That new questions and developments might be
settled and affairs of the church in Constantinople
might be regulated, the Second Ecumenical Council
was convoked by the Emperor Theodosius the Great.
The bishops met in the imperial city in May, 381.[61]
Of this great council F.J.A. Hart is quoted as having
said:

> "In the whole history of the Church
> there is no council which bristles with
> such astonishing facts as the First
> Council of Constantinople. It is one
> of the "undisputed General Councils,"
> one of the four which St. Gregory said
> he revered as he did the four holy
> Gospels, and he would be rash indeed
> who denied its right to the position it
> has so long occupied..."[62]

Though the Council proved to be very significant,
there are some peculiar facts about it which are
worthy of consideration. It was not intended to
be an ecumenical council. It was a local gathering
of only 150 bishops. It was not summoned by the
Pope, nor was he invited. No diocese of the West
was represented, nor the See of Rome or any other
see. It was a council of saints remarkable for
their holiness, zeal, learning, and the eminence of
their sees. It was presided over at first by
Meletius, bishop of Antioch, who was not in communion
with Rome. Meletius died during the session and
was later canonized as a Saint. The Council's
second presiding officer was Gregory Nazianzen,
then "liable to censure for a breach of the canons
which forbade his translation to Constantinople."
"Its action in continuing the Meletian Schism was
condemned at Rome, and its Canons rejected for a
thousand years." The canons were not placed after
the canons of Nice in the Eastern codex, nor was the
creed read at the Council of Ephesus, fifty years
later. The title Second Ecumenical Council is based
on the later universal reception of the council's
creed.63

At the Council, an exclusively oriental gathering,
only adherents to the Nicene party were in attendance.

16

The emperor did not attend. After Gregory resigned as second president, the newly elected patriarch, Nectarius of Constantinople, presided.[64]

The reign of Theodosius gave the second Ecumenical Synod the opportunity to consider the long dispute which had succeeded the First Council; however, it was peaceful in comparison to the former council. The displacement of Arianism by the Nicene orthodoxy had been accomplished, but Athanasianism was still alive.[65]

Athanasius must be lauded for having long stood alone in defending his doctrine of the Trinity, the statement of which proved to be a tremendous product of his efforts. His name will always be associated with this doctrine, though it was not perfected until later. The final agreement was that there is one οὐσία in the Godhead, but there are three hypostases.[66]

This I Council of Constantinople established a decree of faith which is an enlarged form of the Nicene Creed but, originally, without the "Filioque."[67] One theory is that this creed had been used by the Church ten years and was merely incorporated by the Council. The verbal variations in this Nicene-Constantinopolitan Creed agreed with the heresies of Apollinaris and Macedonius. These changes were as follows: Christ was begotten "before all ages...come down from heaven;" He was incarnate "by the Holy Ghost of the Virgin Mary...and was crucified for us under Pontius Pilate;" "and was buried;" "and sitteth at the right hand of the Father;" "again, with glory;" "whose kingdom shall have no end;" and the added words after "I believe in the Holy Ghost."[68] It is here noticed that the confession is enlarged by "an article on the divinity and personality of the Holy Ghost."[69] This added article of confession reads: "And (we believe) in the Holy Ghost...who proceedeth from the Father, who with the Father and the Son together is worshipped and glorified, who spake by the prophets." The creed continues: "And in one holy, Catholic and Apostolic Church. We acknowledge one Baptism for the remission of sins, (and) we look for the resurrection of the dead and the life of

17

the world to come. Amen." [70]

Here it is well to notice that the words "and
the Son," in the above quotation constitute the
Filioque which was added by the Western Church at the
Council of Toledo in 589. This completed the later
doctrines of the Trinity, though it was not accepted
by the Eastern Church. [71]

A comparison of the creeds of the first two
Councils reveals that the Constantinopolitan Creed
omits the anathema which is at the close of the
Nicene Creed; however, it acknowledges the guide of
the Scriptures; it includes the important article
on the Holy Ghost; it states a means to salvation;
it pronounces the virgin birth of Christ. These
statements make it more like the Apostles' Creed.[72]
The important difference in the two creeds, which
cannot be overlooked, is the Creed of Constantinople's
inclusion of the Holy Ghost proceeding from the
Father.

It is interesting and important to note that
there is no evidence of an ecumenical acknowledgement of this creedal enlargement of I Constantinople
until it was read and accepted as Orthodox at the
Council of Chalcedon in 451. [73]

The first canon of the I Council of Constantinople
ratifies the Nicene Creed in its original form and
anathematizes various heresies including Sabellianism
and Arianism.[74] Canon II limits the ministry and
jurisdiction of bishops to their own dioceses. They
are prohibited from going "to churches lying outside
of their bounds." Canon III states, "The bishops of
Constantinople, however, shall have the prerogative
of honour after the Bishop of Rome; because Constantinople is new Rome."[75]   This change effected the
bishops of Antioch and Alexandria, for up until 381
these bishops ranked next to Rome in supreme authority.
This canon places Constantinople second to Rome. The
effect made Constantinople the Rome of the East.
Canon V recognizes the Tome of the Western bishops
which includes the consubstantiality of the Three
Persons.[76]

18

Emperor Theodosius ratified the seven decrees of this council and in 381 enacted a law that provided for the acceptance of all bishops who believed in the Trinity and had fellowship with other orthodox bishops. Though Arianism was destroyed in the Roman empire it persisted among barbarians two centuries longer. This was largely because the barbarians recognized no difference between this doctrine and orthodoxy.[77]

The third ecumenical council convened at Ephesus in 431 having been called by Theodosius II and the Western co-emperor Valentinian III. Presiding over the council was the stern Cyril of Alexandria. Later the number increased to 198 including papal delegates from Rome who were instructed to act as judges over the debates. Though contending for truth this council was guilty of "shameful intrigue, uncharitable lust of condemnation and coarse violence of conduct." The Council's major contribution was a condemnation of the Nestorian heresy, which affirmed the two natures of Christ. The Council of Ephesus affirmed the one person of Christ and that the Virgin Mary should be called "the Mother of God."

It must be admitted that the Council of Ephesus was the least important of the first four Ecumenical Councils because of its negative results. Its condemnation of Nestorianism was not clearly corrected by another specific doctrine.[78]

The Acts of the council reveal that Pope Celestine upon being consulted by Bishop Cyril concerning the heresy of Nestorius, by letter expressed his disapproval of the Nestorian dogma, particularly because Nestorius was unwilling to call the blessed Virgin "Mother of God." Celestine also decrees that Nestorius should be deprived of the episcopate and communion unless within ten days he rejects the innovation. Cyril carried out these plans of the Pope.

Nestorius, the bishop of Constantinople, being a man of considerable influence could have caused much disturbance had not the Emperor written to Cyril suggesting that the doctrine be "examined in a sacred Synod." The decision of the council was to be final.[79]

The prevalent idea of Θεοτόκος (Theotocos)

emphatically stated that if our Lord is God, and if
he was born of the Virgin then the Virgin was
certainly the θεοτόκος ,[80] the "bringer-forth
of God," later implying μητηρθεοῦ, the Mother of God.
Nestorius' answer to this doctrine was that an
impersonal human nature was no human nature, and
that to assert the completeness of Christ's
humanity one must believe that the human person
was united with the divine Person. Du bose quotes
Nestorius: "We will separate the natures and unite
the honor; we will acknowledge a double person and
worship it as one." [81]

It was in November, A.D. 430 that Emperor
Theodosius the Younger summoned the general council
at Ephesus. Due to the delay of several bishops
the synod did not convene until June 22, 431 in the
cathedral at Ephesus named Theotocos.[82]

After the Nicene Creed was read as a standard
of the council,the letters of Cyril and Nestorius
were examined. Nestorius was convinced that he had
in no way departed from the Nicene Creed or orthodox
faith, but the Fathers judged that his letter
disagreed with the Nicene Creed and was censurable.
The papal legates "found all things judged cononically,"
so Nestorius was condemned.[83]

John of Antioch arriving five days later refused
to attend the council but with 39 other bishops
pronounced Cyril and Memnon to be excommunicated.
Cyril held six sessions of the council, which issued
a decree of faith composed of the Nicene Creed
without the Constantinopolitan additions, deposed
John of Antioch and passed six canons, one a condemnation of Pelagianism. Several months later John of
Antioch and Cyril became reconciled and the Council
was accepted as ecumenical.[84]

Nestorius was forced from one place of exile to
another. Enduring the persecutions he wrote an
account of his life entitled "Tragedy." He died
after 439, the place of his death being uncertain.

Canon II of the Council of Ephesus provides for

20

the deposition of any provincial bishops who assents
to or favors Nestorianism. Canon III provides for
the restoration of any clergy who have been forbidden
from the priesthood by Nestorius. Canon IV states
that any clergy who consents to Nestorius or to
Celestius shall be deposed. Canon VI provides for
the excommunication of any layman who resists the
Synod and the discharge of any cleric who does like-
wise. Canon VII alienates any bishop who replaces
the Nicene Creed by another.[85]

   The extreme negativism and lack of doctrinal
reconstruction is very apparent in the Council of
Ephesus; hence, it is the least recognized of the
first four ecumenical councils.

   Twenty years after the Council of Ephesus the
fourth ecumenical council was summoned by Emperor
Marcion. Though Pope Leo wanted it to be in Italy
the council met at Chalcedon in Bithynia, opposite
Constantinople, October 8, 451. The exact number
of bishops present is uncertain, there being between
520 and 630.[86] Next to I Nice, the Council of
Chalcedon was the most important of the general
councils, despite its repudiation by the Monophysites[87]
of the Eastern Church, who were a serious problem.[88]

   The dignity of the council was often interspersed
with verbal and emotional clashes in the discussions,
which lasted fifteen days. One of the major issues
was the point-by-point discussion of Leo's Tome.
Leo had stipulated that the council should make no
new definition of faith, for he assumed it was
determined in his Tome, which was generally accepted.
Marcion resolved that a creedal definition should be
formulated, which would allow for the differences
between the two opposing parties. During the fifth
session the council appointed a commission of twenty-
six bishops to draw up a creed of faith. The formulated creed was unanimously adopted as the orthodox
doctrine of the person of Christ.[89]

   This council began with a recognition of the
acts of the preceding Council of Ephesus making it
ecumenical. It accepted the catholic creed in both
the Nicene and Constantinopolitan forms, assuming

21

that the doctrine of the Trinity needed no further
explanation. An elaborate exposition of the incarnation was made after the council recognized the ex-
positions contained in the letter of Cyril to
Nestorius and the letter of Leo to Flavian, the
former being against Nestorianism, the latter against
Monophysitism.

After considerable vacillation the council
finally passed the symbol of Chalcedon and appended
the Chalcedonian Decrees. The symbol is the
creedal statement of faith with eulogizing of Leo's
Tome. Twenty-eight of thirty proposed canons were
passed, the twenty-eighth being a re-enactment of
the third canon of the I Council of Constantinople.

Pope Leo confirmed the doctrinal confession,
but protested against the twenty-eighth canon, which
made the patriarch of Constantinople equal to him.

Despite the newly formulated doctrine which
was unanimously accepted, the leaders of the Monophysites, followers of Eutyches, continued to arouse
disturbance because of the council's decrees; nevertheless, the emperor, by edicts, gave the force of
law to the council's decisions and ordered the
banishment from the empire of all Euthychians and
the burning of their writings.

At the close of the great council Emperor
Marcius modestly, but impressively, addressed the
bishops almost reproducing the great scene of
Constantine at the close of I Nice. The significance
of the Council of Chalcedon is seen in the fact
that its results have "controlled the faith of the
catholic church from that time to this, with only a
few supplementary and explanatory additions..."[90]

The Tome of St. Leo, his letter to Flavian, which
received important consideration at Chalcedon
contains the following affirmations and comments:
1. Statements against Eutyches as a heretic,
2. the major significance of the three creedal
phrases, "believe in God the Father Almighty, and
in Jesus Christ his only Son and Lord, who was born

22

of the Holy Ghost and the Virgin Mary," 3.
comments on the retention of virginity of the Virgin
Mother, the Holy Ghost giving her the fecundity, 4.
the Savior's perfection and incarnation, 5. Christ
as the Word, 6. the Savior's perfection and incarnation, 5. Christ as the Word, 6. Christ as the
Son of God, and 7. a final attack on Eutyches'
idea of Christ having two natures.[91] This treatise
became one of the most celebrated of patristic
writings.

After the former creeds were sanctioned, the
fifth session of the Council adopted the Symbol of
Chalcedon or the definition of faith. Expressed
almost in the words of Leo's epistle it reads:

> "...Following the holy Fathers we teach
> with one voice that the Son of God and
> our Lord Jesus Christ is to be confessed
> as one and the same Person, that he is
> perfect in Godhead and perfect in man-
> hood, very God and very man, of a reason-
> able soul and (human) body consisting,
> consubstantial with the Father as touch-
> ing his Godhead, and consubstantial with
> us as touching his manhood, made in all
> things like unto us, sin only excepted;
> begotten of his Father before the worlds
> according to his Godhead; but in these
> last days for us men and for our salvation
> born (into the world) of the Virgin Mary,
> the Mother of God, according to his man-
> hood. This one and the same Jesus Christ,
> the only-begotten Son (of God) must be
> confessed to be in two natures, uncon-
> fusedly, immutably, indivisable, inseparably
> united, and that without the distinction
> of natures being taken away by such
> union, but rather...preserved...in one
> Person...one and the same Son and only-
> begotten, God the Word, our Lord Jesus
> Christ...[92]

Following are the main ideas of this symbol:
1. the incarnation of the λόγος or second person
in the Godhead, 2. the precise distinction between

23

"nature" and "person", 3. the incarnation's infinite result is "God-Man," not a double person
but one, 4. the duality of the natures, 5. the
unity of the person, 6. the entire work of Christ
is of his person, and of the "enhypostasia," the
impersonality of the human nature of Christ.[93]

It must be noted that the above creed does not
contain the complete doctrine of the Trinity but only
two-thirds of it. The Christology of this recapitulation of St. Leo's Tome is mainly the incarnate Logos who consists of God's nature plus
human nature in only one person, who is both divine
and human.

Canon II of the decrees of the Council of
Chalcedon is an anathema against any clerics who
buy or sell ordinations. Canon III provides that
bishops are to control the erection of monasteries.
No ordinations are to take place in monasteries,
according to Canon VI. Canon XV states that a
deaconess must be at least forty years of age and
will be anathematized if she marries. Monks and
nuns will be excommunicated if they marry, according
to Canon XVI. The epitome of Canon XIX states,
"Twice each year the Synod shall be held wherever
the bishops of the Metropolis shall designate,
and all matters of pressing interest shall be
determined." Canon XXIV provides that monasteries
are to be immovable. As mentioned previously
Canon XXVIII grants equal rank to the bishop of
Constantinople as to the bishop of Rome. Canon XXIX
makes it a sacrilege to degrade a bishop to the
rank of presbyter.[94]

The last three of the seven ecumenical councils
are less important; therefore, less space will be
devoted to them.

The Second Council of Constantinople was
assembled more than a century after Chalcedon. In
553, Emperor Justinian called the council, without
the pope's consent, for the purpose of adjusting
the still prevalent Monophysite question. The
patriarch Eutychius of Constantinople presided over
the synod of 164 bishops. The fifth council was not

24

recognized by many bishops of the West even after
Pope Vigilius reluctantly assented to it, thus causing
a schism between the Pope and some of the bishops
in Upper Italy for a time. Of the Acts, only the
fourteen anathemas remain extant.[95]

The point in question was the "Three Chapters"
concerning Theodore of Mopsuestia, Theodoret's
writings against Cyril, and the letter of Ibas of
Edessa to Maris, the Persian. These letters were
regarded as heretical. Being of Origenistic origin,
they were anathamatized. Fourteen anathemas were
also charged against Origen[96] who died about 300
years before.

In 549, a few years before the council
convened, Pope Vigilius issued his "Judicatum"
against the "Three Chapters." Though the three
men concerned were a part of the Council of
Chalcedon, the Pope managed to save the authority
of the former council. This action resulted in a
temporary excommunication of the pope by the West.
When the Council met in 553 Pope Vigilius, not in
attendance, issued his document, known as the
"Constitution," in which he condemns certain
propositions of Theodore and Theodoret, but he
pronounces Ibas' letter to be orthodox according to
the former Council of Chalcedon.

Despite the Pope's vacillations[97] the Council
decided that the question had been properly raised,
and it declared all three writings to be heretical.
In so doing the council did not spare Vigilius, the
decrees of the sacred council prevailing above
those of the Pontiff.[98] "Notwithstanding the
concessions of the fifth ecumenical council, the
Monophysites remained separated from the orthodox
church...Since that time the history of the Monophysites has been distinct from that of the catholic
church." The monophysite sects are the Jacobites,
Copts, Abyssinians, Armenians and Maronites.[99]

Perhaps the main accomplishments of the II
Council of Constantinople were its fourteen anathemas
against the third century theologian Origen. These
may be readily understood by comparing his views with
the formulated creeds of the earlier councils.[100]

25

The Sixth Ecumenical Council met in November, 680. After eighteen sessions it ended in September, the following year. The number of bishops present was under 300. This Third Council of Constantinople was held under Constantine Progonatus, the Pope being Agatho I. The council proved victorious over the Menothelite view, insofar as one will depends upon one nature.[101]

When the Emperor summoned the council he had no intention that it be ecumenical, but when it assembled, the title of "Ecumenical" was assumed. At this council the emperor presided.[102] Agatho was present and fully in sympathy with the proceedings. This council was noted for "the order and impartiality of its deliberations." A decree of faith was issued asserting the coexistence of the two wills in the one Christ. The Monothelites were condemned and the dead Honorius, former bishop of Rome, was anathematized because of certain of his statements. The main contribution of the Sixth Ecumenical Council was "the assertion of the proper humanity not only the incarnate nature of our Lord, as decided at Chalcedon, but as essential constituents of his activity and will within the nature."[103]

The council's definition of faith includes the following statements concerning both the divinity and humanity of Christ:

> "...Our Lord Jesus Christ must be confessed to be very God and very man, one of the holy and consubstantial and life-giving Trinity, perfect in Deity and in humanity, very God and very man, of a reasonable soul and human body subsisting; consubstantial with the Father as touching his Godhead and consubstantial with us as touching his manhood; in all things like unto us, sin only excepted; begotten of his Father before all ages according to his Godhead..."

The doctrine of dithelitism is also included:

> "...defining all this we likewise declare that in him (Jesus Christ) are two natural

26

wills and two natural operations
indivisibly, inconvertibly, inseparably,
inconfusedly, according to the teaching
of the holy Fathers. And these two wills
are not contrary the one to the other
(God forbid!) as the impious heretics
assert, but his human will follows and
that not as resisting and reluctant,
but rather as subject to his divine and
omnipotent will...For as his most holy
and immaculate animated flesh was not
destroyed because it was deified but
continued in its own state and nature
(ἔρω Τοκαὶ λόγω), so also his human will,
altho' deified, was not suppressed, but
was rather preserved..."

"...we say that his two natures shone
forth in his one subsistence in which he
both performed the miracles and endured
the sufferings thru the whole of his
economic conversation..."[104]

The Seventh Ecumenical Council was the Second Council
of Nice. It was called by the emperor and empress
Constantine VI and Irene in 787. This council
sanctioned the image-worship of the Catholic Church,
but it has no dogmatic significance.

The ecumenical character of this council has
been disputed; however, certain scholars claim that
there is no reason for doubting that II Nice was
ecumenical. Percival in his Introduction to the
material on this council quotes Bell, who lists
several excellent reasons for readily accepting II
Nice as ecumenical. Bell states, "...it would be
strange were anyone to doubt the historical fact
that the Second Council of Nice is one of the
Ecumenical Councils of the Catholic Church, and
indeed so far as I am aware none have done so except
such as have been forced into this position for
doctrinal consistency."[105]

The Acts of the seventh general council include
anathematisms against image breakers, those referring
to images as idols, those who do not salute the

27

venerable images, calling the images gods, and communicating with those who dishonor the images.[106] Other anathemas were passed against those who fail to believe in the Trinity and the various doctrines pertaining to it as seen in the creeds.[107] The decree of faith of the Second Council of Nice is largely a recapitulation of the previously formulated creeds.[108] Twenty-two canons were passed. Canon IV prohibits bishops from receiving gifts. Canon VIII makes special demands on Hebrew converts. Canon IX provides for the destruction of books which are against images. Canon X prohibits any cleric from leaving his diocese without the Bishop's consent. Canon XIII is a special condemnation against those who turn monasteries into public houses. No cleric can serve two churches, according to Canon XV. Canon XVIII prohibits women from living in bishop's houses or monasteries. There are to be no double monasteries, according to Canon XX. [109]

The regulations concerning the images might be better understood in the light of the fact that in the early church, symbols were used quite extensively in the West; however, the Eastern Church did not allow them. II Nice gave universal sanction to the use of images through legislation. It is likely that the Catholic Church used symbols and images or similar items even in the second century. Eusebius' excellent descriptions of the splendor of the affairs and churches indicate this.[110]

V

A progressive creedal development may be traced in the symbols of the ecumenical councils. They contain chiefly the doctrines of orthodoxy -- of God, Christ, the Holy Spirit, the Trinity and the Incarnation. These creeds have been discussed individually, so a comparison of them is in order. This comparison will include a designation of the similarities and differences between the Ecumenical Creeds and the Apostles' Creed.

An understanding of the Apostles' Creed is essential to this comparison. The Apostles' Creed is not the work of the apostles, as was once believed, but an early summary of their teachings. It is in harmony with the New Testament and contains all the essentials of the Christian faith. "It is by far the best popular summary of the Christian faith ever made within so brief a space." Its brevity and simplicity, however, made it insufficient "as a regulator of public doctrine for a more advanced stage of theological knowledge." The Nicene Creed more strongly expresses the divinity of Christ. The later Reformation Creeds are more explicit on the authority and inspiration of the Scripture and the doctrines of sin and grace.

The Apostles' Creed can not be traced to one author, but likely developed from the confession of Peter (Matthew 16:16). The received form of this creed cannot be traced beyond the close of the fifth century. Its original Roman form, as handed down in Latin by Rufinus (390 A.D.) and in Greek by Marcellus (336-341 A.D.), was different from the present text which came into general use in the seventh or eighth century. The additions, as contained in the received form, are the phrases: "Maker of heaven and earth;" "conceived" (by the Holy Ghost); "suffered" (under Pontius Pilate); (crucified) "dead"; "He descended into Hell (Hades);" (right hand of) "God" (the Father) "Almighty;" "I believe" (in the Holy Ghost); "Catholic" (Church); "the communion of saints;" "and the life everlasting."[111]

The following table is a comparison of the received form of the Apostles' Creed with the original Nicene Creed, the enlarged Nicene-Constantinopolitan Creed, the Constantinopolitan Creed and the Chalcedonian Creed:[112]

TABLE I

AP.C. -- Apostles' Creed
E.N.   -- enlarged Nicene Creed of 381 A.D.
O.N.   -- original Nicene Creed of 325 A.D.
C.C.   -- Constantinopolitan Creed of 381 A.D.
( )   -- added later

29

1. AC.P. I believe in God the Father Almighty,
        (Maker of heaven and earth).

    E.N.   We (I) believe in one God the Father
        Almighty, Maker of heaven and earth, And
        of all things visible and invisible.

    O.N.   We believe in one God, the Father Almighty,
        Maker of all things visible and invisible.

    C.C.   We believe in one God, the Father Almighty,
        Maker of (heaven and earth, and of) all
        things visible and invisible.

2. AP.C. And in Jesus Christ, his only Son, our
        Lord;

    E.N.   And in one Lord Jesus Christ, the only-
        begotten Son of God, Begotten of the Father
        before all the worlds; (God of God), Light
        of Light, very God of very God, begotten,
        not made, being of one substance with the
        Father; by whom all things were made.

    O.N.   And in one Lord Jesus Christ, the Son of
        God, begotten of the Father (the only-begotten;
        that is, of the essence of the Father, God of
        God), Light of Light, very God of very God,
        begotten, not made, being of one substance
        with the Father; by whom all things were made
        (both in heaven and on earth);

    C.C.   And in one Lord Jesus Christ, the (only-
        begotten Son of God, begotten of the Father
        (before all worlds), Light of Light, very God
        of very God, begotten, not made, being of one
        substance with the Father; by whom all things
        were made;

3. AP.C. Who was (conceived) by the Holy Ghost,
        Born of the Virgin Mary;

    E.N.   Who, for us men and for our salvation, came
        down from heaven, and was incarnate by the Holy
        Ghost* of the Virgin Mary, and was made man;

*   This phrase is included only in the enlarged Nicene
    Creed.

30

O.N.   who for us men, and for our salvation,
       came down and was incarnate and was made
       man;

C.C.   who for us men and for our salvation,
       came down (from heaven), and was incarnate
       (by the Holy Ghost of the Virgin Mary), and
       was made man;

4. AP.C. (Suffered) under Pontius Pilate, was
          crucified (dead) and buried; (he descended
          into Hades);

    E.N.   He was crucified for us under Pontius
           Pilate; and suffered and was buried;

    O.N.   he suffered

    C.C.   he (was crucified for us under Pontius
           Pilate, and) suffered, (and was buried),

5. AP.C. The third day he rose again from the dead;

    E.N.   And the third day he rose again, accord-
           ing to the Scriptures;

    O.N.   and the third day he rose again,

    C.C.   and the third day he rose again, (accord-
           ing to the Scriptures),

6. AP.C. He ascended into heaven, and sitteth at
           the right hand of (God) the Father (Almighty);

    E.N.   And ascended into heaven, and sitteth at
           the right hand of the Father;

    O.N.   ascended into heaven;

    C.C.   and ascended into heaven, (and sitteth at
           the right hand of the Father);

7. AP.C. From thence he shall come to judge the
           quick and the dead.

    E.N.   And he shall come again, with glory, to
           judge the quick and the dead; whose kingdom

shall have no end.

O.N.   from thence he shall come to judge the
quick and the dead.

C.C.   from thence he shall come (again, with
glory), to judge the quick and the dead;
(whose kingdom shall have no end).

8. AP.C.   and (I believe) in the Holy Ghost.

E.N.   and (I believe) in the Holy Ghost, the
Lord, and Giver of Life; who proceedeth
from the Father (and the Son); who with
the Father and the Son together is glorified;
who spake by the Prophets.

O.N. and in the Holy Ghost

C.C.   And in the Holy Ghost, (the Lord and Giver
of Life, who proceedeth from the Father, who
with the Father and the Son together is
worshiped and glorified, who spake by the
prophets.)

9. AP.C.   The holy (catholic) Church; (the communion
of saints);

E.N.   And (I believe) in one holy catholic and
apostolic church;

O.N.   ---

C.C.   (In one holy catholic and apostolic Church);

10. AP.C.   The forgiveness of sins;

E.N.   We (I) acknowledge one baptism for the
remission of sins;

O.N.   - - -

C.C.   (we acknowledge one baptism for the remission of sins);

32

11. AP.C. The resurrection of the flesh (body)'

    E.N. And we (I) look for the resurrection of the dead;

    O.N. ---

    C.C. (we look for the resurrection of the dead),

12. AP.C. (And the life everlasting).

    E.N. And the life of the world to come.

    O.N. ---

    C.C. (and the life of the world to come).

    O.N. adds: (But those who say: 'There was a time when he was not;' and 'He was not before he was made;' and 'He was made out of nothing' or 'He is of another substance' or 'essence,' or 'The Son of God is created,' or 'changeable,' or 'alterable' -- they are condemned by the holy catholic and apostolic Church).

The above four compared creeds may be compared to the Creed of Chalcedon:

We, then, following the holy Fathers, all with one consent, teach men to confess one and the same Son, our Lord Jesus Christ, the same perfect in Godhead and also perfect in manhood; truly God and truly man, of a reasonable (rational) soul and body; consubstantial (co-essential)with the Father according to the Manhood; in all things like unto us, without sin; begotten before all ages of the Father according to the Godhead, and in these latter days, for us and for our salvation, born of the Virgin Mary, the Mother of God, according to the Manhood; one and the same Christ, Son, Lord, Only-begotten, to be acknowledged in two natures, inconfusedly, unchangeable, indivisibly, inseparably; the distinction of natures being by no means taken away by the union, but rather the property of each nature being preserved, and concurring in one Person and one Subsistence, not

parted or divided into two persons, but one and the
same Son, and only begotten, God the Word, the Lord
Jesus Christ; as the prophets from the beginning
(have declared) concerning him, and the Lord Jesus
Christ himself has taught us and the Creed of the
holy Fathers has handed down to us.

It goes almost without saying that the two
Christian doctrines and studies most affected by way
of interpretation in the councils were the Trinity
and Christology. The most basic concern was the
relationship between the Father and the Son; only
later was the person of the Holy Spirit brought
into the interpretation of the Godhead.

Arius oviously believed in the Son as Logos
but as inferior to the Father or not co-equal with
the Father in the Godhead. While it should be
reasonable to allow for an element of inferiority on
the part of a Son who prays to the Father, the
danger, from the orthodox perspective, lies in the
Arian subordination of the Son as inferior in
essence and not one in nature with the Father. To
express it differently, the orthodox perspective
so much as says that a functional subordination is
not necessarily an essential subordination. The
same applies in principle to the Arian view that
"the Father begot the Son," who, therefore, had a
type of beginning, a matter to which even Origin in
the third century was sensitive. When we think in
terms of the incarnation of the Son there is also an
element of a beginning, yet in neither the case of
the Son nor the incarnation,therefore,need we think
that the divine nature or substance of the Son of
God had a beginning; rather, it can be thought
that the form of the Logos-Son and the incarnate
Christ had beginning(s). In principle this
distinction draws upon the old scholastic differentiation between substance and form.

Another way of putting this matter is to see
the Godhead as one in being essence but with two
(for the immediate issue) and three (for the fuller
picture) modes of divine being. These three "modes"
of divine being, basic to the trinity, are essentially
the same as the "forms" of the essence of the Godhead
or what to the councils are the persons or hypostases.
Karl Barth has provocatively suggested this idea of
the three modes of divine being.[113] The term 'mode'
or 'modes' seems a propos, because it is less stilted

rationalistically than such terms as "substances" or "hypostases." "Modes" convey something of an adaptibility on the part of the Godhead if not a greater elasticity or, better, a more dynamic or pneumatic quality of the divine nature.

The chief problem of interpretation on the part of the councils was the matter of the rational Greek forms of expression. What was being interpreted was extremely important both to Christian theology, and Church unity, but the philosophical method and concepts often were stiff and unbending, hardly lending themselves to the dynamic concepts derived from the scriptures.

The subordinationism theory of Arius not only accentuated the subordinate role of the Son to the Father, a matter not so serious in itself functionally, but it detracted from the equality of the Son with the Father essentially, so as to create in men's minds a notion of a subordinate, if not separate, essence. It might be said that the Logos-Son was made to appear from rather than of the one divine essence. This led many churchmen to think Arius' interpretation smacked of polytheism. To a certain extent Arianism approached what was called Sabellianism, the view basic to a later Unitarianism, which keeps the Son subordinate to the Father. Arius claimed that the Son was different in nature from the Father. This was the core of the conflict. To be different in function and even personhood was one thing; to be different in essence quite another; hence, the pertinence of the issue between "like" in nature versus "same" in nature. One smiles today at the thought of the laymen of that day discussing the theological issues in barber shops of the period and pulling each others' beards in debate over homoousios versus homoiousios. Yet the attempt to rationally resolve the difference between "same" and "like" natures, was no small matter.

The Nicene Creed was the first to articulate the unity of essence between the Father and the Son, a matter also essential to the incarnation's element of divinity. The I Council of Constantinople did much the same with respect to the Holy Spirit as the third person of the Godhead, who proceeds from both the Father and the Son. Eventually, the doctrine of the trinity took shape with the articulation of one nature in the Godhead with three persons treated as hypostases. Yet it seems important to concede that the manipulation of such an abstract concept as "hypostasis" hardly does justice to whatever is meant by "person." While the three-in-one principle of the trinity is kept very much alive, protecting the consubstantiality of the three persons, the question still proves pertinent as to what exactly three persons-in-one divine essence really means. Surely, there is a need today to think in more dynamic terms, i.e. terms that represent the divine Pneuma, and when this is the case it is dubious that rationalistic Greek concepts can do them full justice. The Barthian "modes" of Being are an improvement. Even so, it must be conceded that the members of the ecumenical councils were men of their day who found it necessary to communicate in the philosophical parlance of their day. They were seeking to be intelligible in terms that the Hellenic intelligentsia of the period could understand and appreciate. Unquestionably, it was an early case of philosophy being "the handmaiden of theology."

Sometimes it is said that the doctrine of the trinity is non-scriptural. Surely that is true if you limit the trinity to the precise creedal formula that the councils came up with, however, the basic spirit and precept of the trinity is scriptural if we no more than look to I John 5:1ff. I John is an epistle that alludes frequently to the interrelated roles of the Father, Son and Holy Spirit. In I John 5:7 (K.J.V.) the apostle overtly speaks of the three heavenly witnesses, though it is toned down in more recent translations; nevertheless, many other scriptural passages give foundations for the later formulation of the trinitarian doctrine. Some of the most specific are the following: Matthew 28:19; Luke 3:22; John 1: 1ff; 7:16, 17, 26; 15:26; Galatians 4:4, 6; II Corinthians 13:14. Colossians 1:15ff; Hebrews 1:2, 3; Titus 3:4, 5. Even the modern translations of I John 5:5-9 preserve the spirit of what is germane to the trinity.

This gives evidence that all three of the
persons are represented in the scriptures from time
to time, though seldom fully interrelated in a
single expression and certainty not articulated
definitively in a rationalistic manner. Unless one
is catering to a naive form of polytheism or a
Sabellianism that minimizes the unity and co-
equality of the three persons, the doctrine of the
trinity still appears most congenial to the intent
of the scriptures. For us to take this seriously
today, however, might very well call for a reiteration
of the Barthian idea of the three modes of one
divine Being. Viewed pneumatically, this enhances
the intelligibility of the trinity doctrine and
modifies discreetly the stilted rationalistic forms
of expression used by the councils. To assert
this in no way abrogates what the councils intended
but rather qualifies it dynamically so as to be
less stiff and formal in doctrinal format. Perhaps
had the conveners been more poetic in their methods
of reasoning - - i.e. more in tune with most scriptural styles of thinking, they would have been less
scholastic and sterile in their reasoning. To
assert this is not to say they were remiss, but
it is to be sensitive to the need for a less
restrictive type of reasoning as related to the
three persons. Again, this is not an abrogation
but a qualification of the work of the councils.

The qualification herein contended lends itself
more to the divine nature as pneuma, dynamos and
agape, which according to the New Testament are
dynamic qualities intrinsic to the divine nature
revealed through Christ. The human factor of
ratio does not do justice to these qualities, yet
it was ratio that was fundamental to the methods
of communication and contention used by the council
members. Not that human reason should be displaced
but rather enlarged upon more in keeping with a
holistic view of the interpreter. Such a qualification
might serve to remind the interpreter that even the
best of reasoning on the part of the best of
reasoners is still finite and cannot do full justice
to the infinite even as revealed. If it were, the
scriptures themselves likely would have been written
more definitively or rationalistically.

Though Christology was subordinate to the major concerns of the councils, the work of the councils very much involved Christology, because of the incarnate God implied in the doctrine of the Son. Even Athanasius, the champion of Nicene orthodoxy conceded that the incarnation was a "paradox." He overtly spoke of "the divine dilemma and its solution in the incarnation" and saw it as more than a rational concept.[114] It appears, however, that the councils were prone to overlook this upon treating the persons and doctrines of the Godhead, rationalistically. Adolf Harnack was not altogether wrong in questioning the sagacity of the Church Fathers when they imposed Greek ontological categories upon Christian theology;[115] however, he was wrong in asserting that they Hellenized the Gospel and thereby secularized it. In being communicative with Hellenic thought, it cannot be said that the Fathers obscured the New Testament faith. They simply expressed it in thought forms not typical of the scriptures.

Contrary to Karl Barth's earlier Nestorianism adapted to a temporally Docetic view of Christ,[116] on the one hand, and to modern immanental views of the historical Jesus akin to Harnack's view, on the other, we must assert the full divinity and full humanity of Christ's dual nature. This cannot avoid the both/and paradox of unity-in-duality; eternity-in-time; the Word-made-flesh crystallized in the words: "God was in Christ."[117] This is neither a synthesis nor a dichotomy but a both/and paradox; neither total transcendence nor total immanence does it justice, for it implies elements of both. Dialectically, what is basic is the dynamic paradox of the God-man that addresses itself to the existential paradox of man, redeeming him in relation to, yet from beyond, himself. In speaking of "paradox" Athanasius was not oblivious to this dynamic qualification of the councils' rationalistic endeavors. In conclusion, this dynamic qualification of the councils' endeavors is not an abrogation of their much-needed accomplishments but rather a fulfillment, a manner of thinking that is more composite while not displacing the rational methods used by the councils.

BIBLIOGRAPHICAL FOOTNOTES

1. Montanists were an ascetic type of Christians of the middle second century who emphasized the miraculous gifts of the apostolic Church and proclaimed the age of the Holy Ghost and that the millenial reign had been established in the village of Pepuza in Phrygia, which they termed the New Jerusalem. They deemed themselves the only genuine spiritually-minded Christians and all others carnally-minded. See: McClintock and Strong, Biblical, Theological, and Ecclesiastical Cyclopedia, vol. VI, p.526 ff.
2. Hastings, Encyclopedia of Religion and Ethics, vol. IV, p.185ff. Schaff-Herzog Encyclopedia of Religious Knowledge, vol. III, p.279ff. Encyclopedia Brittanica, 14th ed., vol 6, p.589ff.
3. Percival, Henry R., General Introd., The Nicene and Post-Nicene Fathers, vol. XIV, p.xi.
4. Ibid.
5. J. Wilhelm, Catholic Encyclopedia, vol. IV, p.424.
6. Common feeling or thought.
7. Percival, Henry R., op. cit., p.xii.
8. Ibid., pp. xii, xiii.
9. Ecclesiastical right.
10. By divine right.
11. Monothelism is the doctrine of Christ having two natures but one will.
12. Percival, Henry R., op. cit., pp. xii, xiv.
13. Ibid., p. xxi.
14. Bright, "Notes on Canons", The Nicene and Post-Nicene Fathers, vol. XIV, pp.9,10. See: below for writings here referred to.
15. Perkins, Clarence, Ancient History, p.630.
16. Du bose, William P., The Ecumenical Councils, p.xix.
17. Perkins, Clarence, op. cit., p.631.
18. Du bose, William P., op. cit.
19. Eusebius, "Life of Constantine", The Nicene and Post-Nicene Fathers, vol. I, I: xxviii (see also chs. xxi to xxxii).
20. Socrates, Ecc. Hist., The Nicene and Post-Nicene Fathers, vol. II, I: ii.
21. Foakes-Jackson, F. J., Studies in the Life of the Early Church, p.240f.
22. Du bose, W. P., op. cit. p.xxi.
23. See: Theodoret, Ecc. Hist., The Nicene and Post-Nicene Fathers, vol. IV, Ch. I.

24. Du bose, Wm. P., op. cit. p.33ff.
25. Socrates, Eccles. Hist., op. cit., I: V.
26. See: Jerome, "Lives of Illustrious Men", ch. liv.,
    The Nicene and Post-Nicene Fathers, vol.III.
    See: Footnote 96.
27. Du bose, Wm. P., op. cit., pp. xxiii-xxv.
28. See: Socrates, Eccles. Hist., op cit., I: vi-vii.
29. Merrill, E. T., Essays In Early Christian History,
    p. 250.
30. Ibid., p.251 f.
31. Eusebius, Life of Constantine, op. cit., III: v.
32. Schaff, Philip, History of the Christian Church,
    vol. 3, p.349. See: Eusebius, Life of Constantine,
    op. cit., III: vi.
33. Schaff, Philip, op. cit. p.349.
34. See: Eusebius, op. cit., III: x
35. Sozomenus, Ecc. Hist. I:16, 17, The Nicene and
    Post-Nicene Fathers, vol. II.
36. Socrates, Ecc. Hist., op cit., I: 8
37. Theodoret, Ecc. Hist., I: 1 The Nicene and Post-
    Nicene Fathers, vol. III.
38. See: Sozomenus, op. cit.
39. Du bose, Wm. P., op cit., p. xxvf. Cf. Sheldon,
    Henry C., History of Christian Doctrine, vol. I.
    p. 197ff.
40. Du bose, Wm. P., op. cit., p.xxvi.
41. Schaff, Philip, op. cit., p.349.
42. The Seven Ecumenical Councils, The Nicene and Post-
    Nicene Fathers, vol. XIV, p.3.
43. Du bose, William P., op. cit., p.xxvii.
44. Schaff, Philip, op. cit., p.349, 350, 631.
45. Merrill, E. T., op. cit., p.253.
46. See: The Nicene Creed, The Nicene and Post-
    Nicene Fathers, op. cit., vol. XIV, p.3.
47. See: The Synodical Letter, Council of Nice,
    The Nicene and Post Nicene Fathers, vol. XIV, p.53.
48. Schaff, Philip, op. cit., p.350.
49. See: Canons, Council of Nice, The Nicene and
    Post-Nicene Fathers, vol. XIV, p.8ff.
50. Du bose, Wm. P., op. cit., p.xxvii,Merrill,E.T.,p.261
51. See: Epitome of Canon VI, The Nicene and Post-
    Nicene Fathers, vol. XIV, p.15.
52. Canons, op. cit., p.40
    See: Eusebius, Ecc. Hist., VII: 27-30, The
    Nicene and Post-Nicene Fathers, vol. I.
53. Canons, I-V; IX; XII; XV; XV-XIX, op. cit.
54. Canons, IV-VIII; X-XIV; XX, op. cit.

55. Du bose, William P., op. cit., p.xxvii.
56. Schaff, Philip, op. cit., p.372.
57. Du bose, Wm. P., op. cit., p. xxviii.
58. Eusebius, Life of Constantine, op. cit., III: 16, 17, 20' IV: 47.
59. Schaff, Philip, op. cit., pp. 630, 631.
60. Merrill, E. P., op. cit., p.252.
61. Du bose, Wm. P., op. cit., p.xxix.
62. "Historical Introduction", The Seven Ecumenical Councils, The Nicene and Post-Nicene Fathers, vol. XIV, p.162.
63. Ibid.
64. Schaff, Philip, op. cit., p.350.
65. Du bose, Wm. P., op. cit., p.162.
66. Ibid. p.164.
67. Cf. p. 13; See: "The Seven Ecumenical Councils," op.cit., p.165.
68. The Constantinopolitan Creed, Nicene and Post-Nicene Fathers, vol. XIV, p.163. Cf. Nicene Creed, op. cit.
69. Schaff, Philip, op. cit., p.350.
70. The Constantinopolitan Creed, op. cit.
71. Hastings, Encyclopedia of Religion and Ethics.
72. Schaff, Philip, Creeds of Christendom, vol. I, p.25ff.
73. See: Canons and Excursus, Nicene and Post-Nicene Fathers, vol. XIV, p.177ff.
74. Ibid, p.176.
75. Ibid, p.178.
76. Ibid, p.181.
77. Schaff, Philip, History of the Christian Church, vol. III, p.640.
78. Ibid, pp. 348, 350.
79. "Historical Introd." The Seven Ecumenical Councils, op. cit., p.192f.
80. See: "Excurses," Council of Ephesus, Nicene and Post-Nicene Fathers, vol. XIV, p.206ff. See: Suetonius, Lives of the Caesars, pp. 228, 229. It becomes noteworthy that the "Mother of God" idea was not originally Christian. Suetonius, the great Roman writer and historian of the second century, in his biography of Octavius Augustus speaks of "a priest of the Mother of the Gods." This concept was originally pagan. In the Greek and Roman mythology, Cybele or Rhea was pronounced the "Mother of the Gods." For more information on this subject, see:

Gayley, Classic Myths; Fowler, Roman Myths; Harper, Dictionary of Classical Antiquities.

81. Du bose, Wm. P., op. cit., p. xlix.
82. Ibid, p. li.
83. "Historical Introd." op. cit., pp. 194, 195.
84. Du bose, Wm. P., op. cit., p. liif.
85. Canons, Council of Ephesus, The Seven Ecumenical Councils, The Nicene and Post-Nicene Fathers, vol. XIV, p. 225ff.
86. Schaff, Philip, op. cit., p.351. Du bose, Wm. P., op. cit., p.lixf.
87. Monophysites: Believers in the theological and metaphysical doctrine of the one nature of Christ. Followers of Eutyches.
88. Schaff, Philip, op. cit., p. 351.
89. Du bose, Wm. P., op. cit., pp. lxf; 252.
90. Ibid, pp. lxif; 252f and Schaff, Philip, op. cit., pp. 351ff, 740ff.
91. The Tome of St. Leo, The Nicene and Post-Nicene Fathers, pp. 254-258.
92. "The Definition of Faith of the Council of Chalcedon," The Nicene and Post-Nicene Fathers, vol. XIV, pp. 262-265.
93. Schaff, Philip, op. cit., pp. 750-762.
94. Canons of Chalcedon, The Nicene and Post-Nicene Fathers, vol. XIV, pp. 266-292.
95. Schaff, Philip, op. cit., p.351f.
96. Origen believed God to be absolute having no greater or lesser, higher or lower. To him God is Monad, Unit, Mind; God is incorporeal. Yet Origen avoids pantheism. God is spaceless, timeless, everywhere and nowhere, unchangeable, without feelings, yet merciful having the passion of Love. Origen also believed God to be not infinite but self-limiting; His almightiness being limited by His goodness; not culpable. Intimate knowledge of God is by revelation, not abstraction.
   With respect to the Trinity, Origen maintained that the Logos or Son is center of the Godhead, being co-eternal and co-equal with the Father. There never was a time when He was not. The Person of the Holy Spirit is co-eternal and co-equal with the Father and Son. Though he questioned whether the Holy Spirit came into being through the Word (διὰ τοῦ λο) οῦ εγένετο

or whether He has no separate essence,
(ἕτέραν οὐσίαν) from the Father and Son,
Origen was not a subordinationist.
   Origen was not raised to sainthood by the
Catholic Church, because his concept of the
Trinity was not as later established.
See: Hastings, Encyclopedia of Religion and
Ethics.

97.   This surely does not render favor to the idea
      of papal infallibility.
98.   "Hist. Introd.", II Constantinople, The
      Nicene and Post-Nicene Fathers, vol. XIV,
      pp. 299-300.
99.   Schaff, Philip, op. cit., pp. 771f. See:
      Du bose, William P., op. cit., p.275ff.
             Note: The Armenians are not to be
      confused with the later Arminians.
100. See: note 96. Compare with the creed of the
      councils. See: Anathema Against Origen,
      The Nicene and Post-Nicene Fathers,
      vol. XIV, pp. 318-320.
101. Schaff, Philip, op. cit., p.771f.
102. "Hist. Introd.", Third Council of Constantinople,
      The Nicene and Post-Nicene Fathers, vol. XIV,
      p. 326.
103. Du bose, Wm. P., op. cit., pp. lxixf, 289.
104. The Definition of Faith, III Constantinople,
      Nicene and Post-Nicene Fathers, vol. XIV,
      p. 344ff.
105. Introduction, II Nice, Nicene and Post-Nicene
      Fathers, vol. XIV, p.522ff.
106. Extracts from the Acts, Nicene and Post-Nicene
      Fathers, vol. XIV, p.533ff.
107. Ibid, p.545.
108. Ibid, p.549.
109. Canons of II Nice, Nicene and Post-Nicene
      Fathers, vol. XIV, pp.555-570.
110. Eusebius, Eccles. Hist., X:4, op. cit., and Life
      of Constantine, III: 48, 50, op. cit.
111. Schaff, Philip, Creeds of Christendom. vol.I,
      pp. 14-23.
112. Creeds as found in vols. I and II of Creeds of
      Christendom by Schaff.
113. Karl Barth, Die Menschlichkeit Gottes; The Faith
      of the Church

44

114. Athanasius, The Incarnation of the Word,
      Macmillan, N.Y., 1946, par. 16, 17, 18, p.4ff.
      Athanasius likewise speaks of the resurrection
      as a "mighty paradox." par. 24, p.54.
115. Adolf Harnack, The History of Dogma, Vol. I.
      Actually, Edwin Hatch asserted this in his
      Hibbert Lectures of 1888, The Influence of
      Greek Ideas on Christianity, p.332.
116. Karl Barth, Die Kirchliche Dogmatik, Band II,
      halbband 1, pp. 694f; 165,167ff, 180, 188.
117. Cf. my book, The Paradox of Existentialist
      Theology, pp. 197-204, also my books Time And
      Its End, pp. 135ff, 216ff, 267ff, and The
      Arminian Arm of Theology, p. 123ff.

BIBLIOGRAPHY

Athanasius, The Incarnation of The Word, New York: Macmillan, 1946.

Barth, Karl, Die Kirchliche Dogmatik, Band I, II, Zurich: Evangelisher Verlag, Edit.8,1960-65.

Barth, Karl, Die Menschlichkeit Gottes, Zeilikon-Zurich: Evangelischer Verlag, 1956.

Barth, Karl, The Faith of the Church, New York: Meridian Books Inc., 1958.

Du bose, William P., The Ecumenical Councils, third ed., New York: Charles Scribner and Sons. 1900.

Eusebius, Ecclesiastical History, The Nicene and Post-Nicene Fathers, second series, vol I, editors Schaff and Wace, New York: The Christian Literature Co., 1890.

Eusebius, "The Life of Constantine," The Nicene and Post-Nicene Fathers, second series, vol. I, editors Schaff and Wace, New York: The Christian Literature Co., 1890.

Foakes-Jackson, F. J., Studies in the Life of the Early Church, New York: Geo. H. Doran Co., 1924.

Harnack, Adolf, The History of Dogma, Vol. I, Boston: Beacon Press, 1957.

Hatch, Edwin, The Influence of Greek Ideas on Christianity, New York: Harper & Bros., (1888), 1957.

Jerome, Lives of Illustrious Men, The Nicene and Post-Nicene Fathers, second series, vol. III. editors Schaff, Wace, New York: The Christian Literature Co., 1882.

Merrill, E. T., Essays in Early Christian History, London: Macmillan Co., 1924.

Perkins, Clarence, Ancient History. New York: Harper and Bros., 1936.

Schaff, Philip, Creeds of Christendom, vol. I,
New York: Harper and Bros., 1884.

Schaff, Philip, Creeds of Christendom, vol. II,
New York: Harper and Bros., 1884.

Schaff, Philip, History of the Christian Church.
vol. III, New York: Charles Scribner and Sons,
1891-1892.

Sheldon, Henry C., History of Christian Doctrine.
vol. I, New York and London: Harper and Bros.,
1901.

Slaatte, Howard A., Time And Its End, Washington,
D.C.: University Press of America, (1961), 1980.

Slaatte, Howard A., The Paradox Of Existentialist
Theology, New York: Humanities Press, 1971.

Slaatte, Howard A., The Arminian Arm of Theology,
Washington, D.C.: University Press of America, 1977.

Socrates, Ecclesiastical History, The Nicene and
Post-Nicene Fathers, second series, vol. II,
editors Schaff and Wace, New York: The Christian
Literature Co., 1890.

Sozomenus, Ecclesiastical History, The Nicene and
Post-Nicene Fathers, second series, vol.II, editors
Schaff and Wace, New York: The Christian Literature
Co., 1890.

Suetonius, The Lives of the Caesars, English translation by J. C. Rolfe, vol. I of Loeb Classical
Library, New York: Macmillan Co.

Theodoret, Ecclesiastical History, The Nicene and
Post-Nicene Fathers, second series, vol. III, IV
New York: The Christian Literature Co., 1892.

The Seven Ecumenical Councils, The Nicene and Post-
Nicene Fathers, second series, vol. XIV, editors
Schaff and Wace, New York: Charles Scribner and
Sons, 1900.

Encyclopedia Brittanica. 14th ed., vol. 6
Encyclopedia Brittanica Co., 1936.

Hasting's Encyclopedia of Religion and Ethics,
Vol. IV, New York: Scribner and Sons, 1912.

McClintock and Strong, Biblical, Theological and
Ecclesiastical Cyclopedia, Vol. VI,
New York: Harper and Bros., 1891.

Schaff-Herzog, Encyclopedia of Religious
Knowledge, Vol. III, New York and London:
Funk and Wagnalls Co., 1909.

The Catholic Encyclopedia, vol. IV,
New York: Appleton Co., 1908.

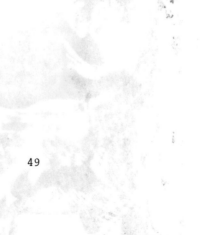